Comforting Clouds

Soft landings for the soul

Divya Subash

Made with ❤ on the BookLeaf Publishing Platform
www.bookleafpub.in
www.bookleafpub.com

"In honour of the little girl I used to be, who found
magic in the sky and to the woman I have become,
who still believes.."

"To those who have ever felt lost in the storm of
life, may these words be your comforting clouds,"

Acknowledgement

I acknowledge the support of all my loved ones, whose unwavering encouragement and understanding enabled me to bring my debut book *Comforting Clouds* to fruition.

I extend my sincere gratitude to my publishers and also appreciate the contributions of the ones who have shared their challenges, difficult times, stories and experiences with me, providing an inspiration for this book.

Preface

Comforting Clouds is a heartfelt collection of thoughts and reflections that embraces the complexities of human experience. This book serves as an invitation to explore the depths of struggles and triumphs. I aim to provide a safe and compassionate space of comfort for readers, to remind them that they are not alone and that they are also a part of this shared journey of life.

My hope is that this little debut book will remind you that your strength lies within you and life's challenges are temporary. As you read these pages, you will find a sense of peace, reassurance, and connection.

1. Poet's Charm

In a world of strange beauty,

Where emotions reside

Her deep thoughts are the threads

That weave her poetic nest..

In solitude, she crafts her creative spell

The charm of words, awakens her dreams.

As words ignite,

A moonlit magic illuminates the sky

Her heart ablaze, she spreads her wings to fly

As poetic beauty unfolds, her spirit takes a flight

Echoing her essence of life,

With a voice that's truly hers.

2. My Own Destiny

As I lift my quill

To script my own destiny,

Strange thoughts arise....

Am I a skilled writer

To write what my heart wishes?

Am I a skilled editor to edit

What my mind commands?

Thoughts begin to drift

Am I in trance hypnotised by

My own dragging dreams?

I become silent for a while...

Are things really destined?

Clash of thoughts flashes

What if this was another play

Of the 'Creator' predestined

For me to write my own destiny

That's already been created???

3. Unwritten Chapters

The visible walls hide invisible stories

Before the unseen becomes visible,

Heal your wounds faster,

Let the fears dissolve

March forward with a heart full of pride;

Each dawn rises with a blank new canvas

Paint it with fearlessness

With brush strokes of inner strength

Embrace this puzzled life

Unlock the inner treasure

When life's journey seems

So far and hidden

Let light prevail,

Even when trials are long

For in depths, your heart

Will guide you, right and strong!

4. The Art of Heartache

The elegant shining crystal ring

Dyed with words of love, was never a pledge

Broken noiseless, the soul forgot its joyous
song to sing

Sorrows like thorn pricks, chaining the pain
on the edge

Oh! Time, it garmented nine

The flame of pain just stood

As he uttered, "Thy, never mine!"

Her soul became a cold waxed wood

The blushing amorous roses shall never bloom

No haven of hope found, it's been years..

Her ballad of joy became a tale of gloom

Faintly echoing a sad song of her lost tears...

5. Web of Perception

We hide behind faces, reflecting the gazes

We've learned to adorn;

We forgive the beloved for every stumble

Yet, the ones we loathe, even virtues

Can't redeem;

We pursue those who scorn us

Seeking validation,

Trapped in this cycle

Chasing approval day and night.

When will we break free from this web?

To some we are radiant, to others

We are a shame;

Our worth measured by love or dislike;

In this web of conditional love

We lose ourselves

We search for acceptance

Yet struggle to give;

Imprisoned in judgements

We conceal our true selves.

6. The Cosmic Balance

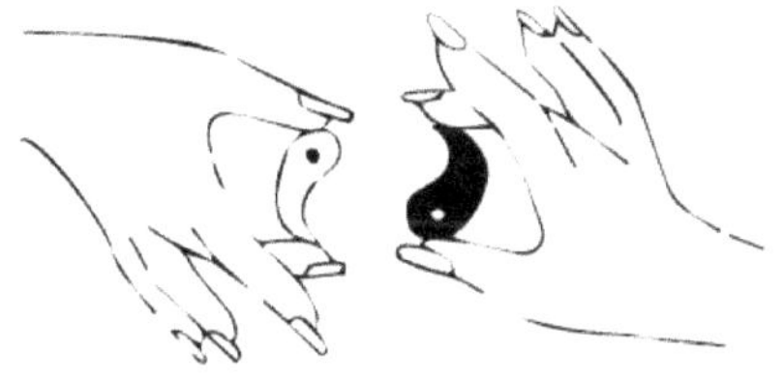

Actions woven, echoes in time

Like seeds planted deep inside

The cosmos keeps the score

The universe decides to harvest

Consequences unfolding, like ripples on water

For each thought and chant

Energy flows in circular way

Like magnetic sway, Karma's wheel

Turns with precision so fine

Deeds radiate wider, in the tides of life

Sown in shadows and harvested in sight

Through trials and tests, we grow

Intensions shape the fate;

Karma's wisdom, mysterious force

Is balancing the scales for me and you.

7. Dis/Connected

In quiet moments, I yearn to be

Alone, wild, and free

No voices, no expectations high

But, then the pangs of loneliness hits

The ache of emptiness, a hollow space

I weigh my desires torn apart

Between solitude's peace

And love's warm heart

My heart, a battlefield of conflicting needs

Torn between solitude's calmness

And love's gentle deeds

In crowded rooms, I feel alone

Like a stranger in my own hollow throne

Is it fear of loss? or fear of gain?

Yet, in this turmoil I search for balance

Embracing this paradox within!

8. Love's Spell

Along the quiet pathway, upon this lovely earth

The flowers you gave me unveiled

A beautiful garden of love within me..

In the miraculous garden of our love

These flowers became my

Macroscopic world of emotions

The gentle wind magically perfumed by

The sweet tenderness of the fragrant flowers

The wide petals reflected our love with pride;

The lands are wide and free, yet

Within your heart my heart finds its home;

In life's turbulent swirls, we sway as one

In mystical dance of joy and tears

Let our hearts hold as one and rejoice in
delight

A love so pure is a celestial wonder;

A love so strong defies all odds;

A magical love awakens the soul and makes us
whole..

It's a miracle that true love's gentleness

Never grows old.

9. Life's Imperfect Harmony

Life's tapestry woven with hellos and goodbyes,

Trapped in the never-ending spin of joys and scars;

Nothing stays the same

Like splashing ocean waves,

Memories ebb and flow

Pain and pleasure entwined forever more

When sorrows creep and ache slowly,

Conceal it gently, calmly thread by thread

Make space for warm light

To unravel the frozen stillness

Let hope seep through

Allow your heart to ponder

Like the monsoon shower

For this beautiful life demands

To be lived and loved boldly.

10. A Life Unnoticed

In quiet moments, I look within

Reflecting on the life, I have lived

No grand achievements

No fame to claim;

Yet, my days are filled with love,

Care and gentleness

No spotlight shines on me.

Just a simple life

I may not have stories of triumph

But in this simple life

I find my pride..

Let my life remain unsung

But, in the love I give

I discover the greatest

Love of all—within me.

11. Beyond the Screen

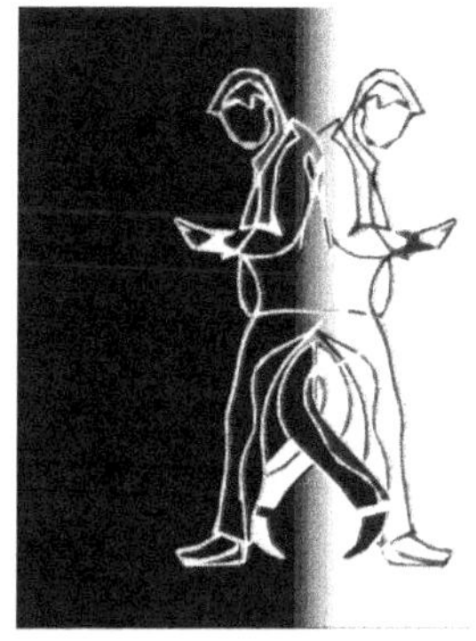

Across the virtual landscapes we gather

Where emojis and shortcuts

Create a vast realm

Connections are made with a click

In the digital space, we find our stage

In this online world, we search for more

Beyond the screen there is a mask hidden

Beneath the sweet words lies truth unspoken

For in digital world, deceit and

False connections can survive

Be wise and cautious too

Let's not forget the world outside too

And safeguard our hearts

Every single day.

12. Still falling Deep

Oh! Wish there were anti-gravity plates

Beneath the earth's ground

To withstand hearts that

Irresistibly fall.....

A wrong love so strong,

Shatters the inner self

Collapsing all into a vaulted box of pain

There's no escape

Beware, for love's sweet trap

Can hold you tight!

It's hard to break free

From it's poison, that spreads so deep

Tread carefully, for your heart

Can become your own burden

A weight that anchors you

To the love's dark endless ocean....

13. Hidden Intentions

Hidden intentions, risen from deep

Gifts grief that's too deep for words!

As disguised words of masked promises

Mock the injuries of sorrows

The raw real colours stiffen the lips..

As grief swells, emotions numb

As if no cup of hope remains..

Heart laments in vain...

Blinded by shadowed trust

Only stillness is left, like frozen snow..

Turning the heart into a mirror

Only to reflect the pain

That will never fade!!!

14. Mind's Turbulence

Mind a maze, thoughts scattered and lost

The familiar becomes uncertain

Like a forgotten memory

Fears and doubts resurface

Clarity dissolves, only confusion remain

A battleground where logic and instinct clash;

A fragile balance like a tightrope walk

Turbulence rages, ceaseless tides

Waves crash on, amidst chaos

A spark of resilience, forged

Let the beacon of hope guide me

The turbulent waters to calmer shores.

15. From Chains to Wings

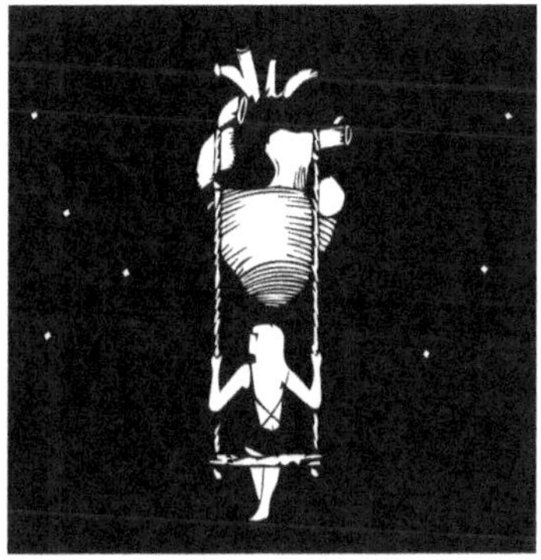

Dwelling on duality's might

Letting go of illusions,

Facing the tides of truth and

Confronting the shadows

Is a tough challenge to conquer

The suffocation of sufferings,

Ignites the inner demons,

Feeding its flames..

Letting go of chained feelings,

Little by little, pacifies the pain

From chains to wings

Break the boundaries

And transcend the limits

To live a liberated life

As light as air, wild and free.

16. Lens Of Reality

With myriad of lifestyle choices available

Just seek to focus through the lens of reality

Inner turmoil brews a storm of emotions

Fueled by life's unmet longings

Stagnation sets in,

Tired of repetition being a mere puppet;

Yet, all are seduced by the glamour of life

Deceived by the societal pressure

Luring us into a borrowed lifestyle

That's not our own....

It's always better to choose

What suits us the best!

Try and cultivate an authentic style

And be that masterpiece that's crafted

Just for you by you...

17. Time's Tender Touch

As time's gentle moments slowly bloom

Memories held in fragile frames of mind

Rekindle a love that's so pure

Quenching the deep longings of the soul

Each breath with you is a joy profound

Together we wander, hand in hand

Through the life's garden

Gathering the petals of joy

Our hearts beating as one in this sweet
collision

Forever entwined in the love's embrace

Wish that time's fleeting wings would pause

To savour the moments and make them last

18. Begin Again

Like a knife in the night

My words cut you deep..

I spilled sorrows' dark ink

In the pages of your heart

The light in your eyes

Slowly dimmed by the

Shadows of my mistake...

Now, tears of regret flow like a river

I long to turn back the time

To seek your forgiveness,

And make things right

I'll bring back your light that once shined

Can you tell me, where to begin again?

How to mend and ease your pain?

The weight of my flaws makes me wonder

If your love for me still remains the same..

19. Hidden Realm

Nature hides magnificent and marvellous
secrets

Intricately connecting the visible patterns
invisibly;

It's a divine paradise, where wisdom awakens

A perfect symphony where beauty sings

A majestical cradle, where tales are told

A secret space of cosmic marvel

Where myths, illusions and fantasies

Mystically merge;

Every pattern is woven with love and care

Each hour is golden

Time after time, season after season

Nature spreads its arms in perfect rhyme

In nature's tender arms, we find our peaceful
rest

In radiant havens, magical mysteries slowly
unfold

Embrace the mystical charm in silence

And bloom in nature's garden,

Completing and complementing the

Tapestry of grand cosmic tales

That once began..

20. Change the Unchangeable

Racial segregation's venomous sting

Poisons the toxic societal opinion.

Sarcasm's sharp blade cuts deep

Destroying the fair dreams....

Depression's dark whisper

Echoing suicide's desperate plea

Frightening, how little this society
understands..

The fleeting glance and nameless hasty sigh

Fuels the aggression;

Let's unite and shatter the ignorance

Let all the hearts open wide..

Survivors are warriors!

May the winds of change begin to blow now

Let those voices of the silenced be heard

For a brighter future dawn,

Change the unchangeable.

21. World of Words

In the pages turned, where minds wander

Our souls find solace in the ink spilled;

Books are our refuge, our shelter

Whispers of love, laughter and tears

Echoes in these spaces, through all years;

Inked words, a heartfelt choice to be our
voice;

A reflection of hope, in times unknown

Within their pages, a paradise unfolds

In every verse, imagination thrives;

Making our hearts rejoice;

With every line, a tale unfolds;

Books, a treasure trove of knowledge

In world of words we find our way

For in the words, we find a piece

Of our soul's deepest longings.

22. The Denial

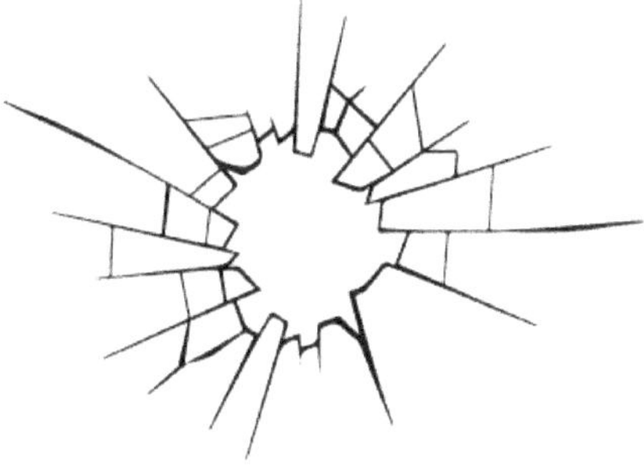

Rejection, a familiar friend

Each "No" a test of might

Denied paths are clear

And when new roads emerge

We fall and fade

Like autumn leaves

The path we walk

Is a trial by flame

Rejections fire,

Strengthens heart

Courage emerges

To reveal a brighter view

Dissolving the weight of doubt

Like a morning dew

Let rejection be the guide and

A stepping stone to other side

Where strength and resilience unite.

23. Luxury Chains

A lavish golden cage encases my soul.

A life of ease, wrapped in chains of gold

Where freedom fades to a distant,

Yet,

Inside the gilded halls, I find a

A love so pure that bounds me tight

I cherish that love, that's truly rare

I deeply desire that this love's pure fire

Will melt the golden chain

Before long,

The bars of gold will become a bridge

Like a ray of hope, a gentle breeze

Guides me forth, to another day

Do blessings feel like chains?

Can wealth's weight hold us captive

While the dreams sleep?

24. Random Errors

In the inked chapters of my life,

I have my own known,

Unknown random errors

Introspective lens is a must

To keep my life graph

Marching towards success

Let not thorns of those

Choke the bloom

My dreams will define me

My efforts will define me

But my errors...

Can never define me or my life

In the end, no one is perfect

To err is human, right?

My uncertainties also shape a path

With every misstep, a lesson unfolds

In the beauty of imperfection,

I discover my own direction..

25. Silent Devotion

I see your gentle face

A fleeting joy, in my lonely space

The ache of longing, I solely embrace

Though you may never call me your own,

Just like a whispered prayer,

My love so true, resides without a voice

Time may pass, seasons may fade

But my devotion forever will stay

Unspoken and unseen..

Though unrequited, like a shadow

I follow and protect you

With silent pride!

My silent love remains forever unknown.

26. River Of Reflection

To unfold thousands of dreams,

I look deeper into the depths of my soul,

A tear fell to tickle a ripple,

Only to collide with the invisible darkness

That exists in me, just as the river;

I surface my reflection on its calm surface

A magnetic smile reappears,

Hiding the depths of my inner sea..

Fearless rivers swiftly flow like a poet's verse

I am the river, pulsing with a heartbeat

I am the river, a river of untamed emotions

I sail through the turbulent tides of
transformation

Where life's waves crash and reshape

I will soon find my own rhythm and flow..

27. Spectrum Of Wonder

A magical majestic arc

With gentle curves,

A vibrant bow softly glowing,

Woven with a touch of grace

A harmonious spectrum

Red ignites, Orange glows

Yellow shines, Green soothes

Blue blooms, Indigo whispers

Violet dreams like a magical spell

Merging together and adorning the sky,

Like a symbol of promise

That life is a colourful ride.

28. The Silent Language

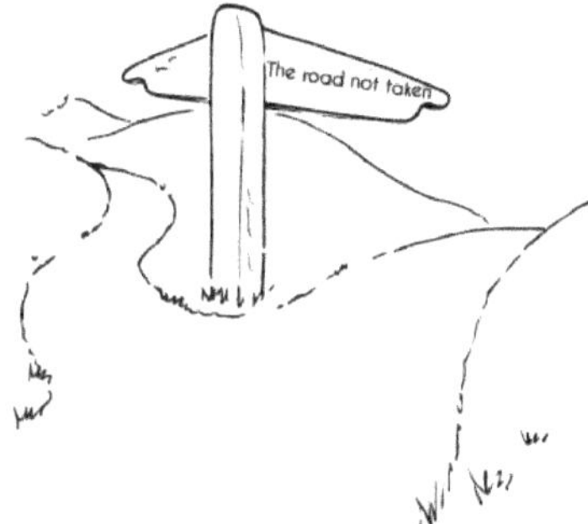

Two paths converge, a single road

Where words fail, hearts take the lead

Softly our soul connects,

A language of love, only we need

A promise is made,

Deepening our connection

With each passing day

In every step, a love blooms

Radiant, timeless, and forever true

In each other's eyes, a home we find

Our hearts entwine forever

Sealed with love

That's meant only for us.

29. Limitless Horizon

Trapped beneath the locked blue shell,

Thoughts whisper secrets

Some twisted in complexity, others wild...

A spectrum of frustration and

Missed opportunities threaten to consume..

Pushing to the edge,

Where fears and doubts collide

Is there a way to shatter the chains?

Unlock the chaos to unblock the mind

Face the shadows that haunt

Dare to look up and see..

Sky is just an illusion of limit

Fly beyond and seize your throne

Ignite the fire and let your spirit soar...

30. Inner Shore

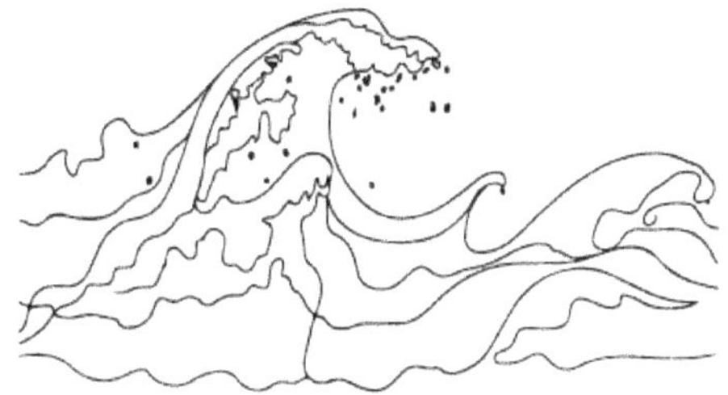

The ocean's rhythm synchronises with our souls

Flowing with life's emotional currents

A vast and mysterious expanse

Concealing secrets and stories

In the depths much like our minds

Unseen, unknown relentless roar

The ocean's power stirs

Courage to leave the fears

Its serenity calms our mind

It reminds us to just

Flow, adapt, and let go

And embrace the beauty

Of the unknown..

31. Mirrors Reflection

In silvered glass,

My new reflection stares

As monologue unwinds

Whispers of transformation rise

I shed the old skin,

With awakened eyes

Within its depth,

The real story unfolds

As I gaze in the mirror

A journey starts

To find my true self,

Leaving the past behind

In this reflection,

My new self is born

32. Saviour's Embrace

A heart of kindness, melts the cold ache

Healing me anew.

Beyond the wall, illusions spin

Yet, my saviour's love

Rescues my hope within

In me a spark of light is alive

Faith restored, beliefs revived

Strength renewed, I rise again

A symbol of hope,

In this refuge, I find my peace.

33. The World Beyond Words

Embrace the magic of monsoon

Lift your face to face the rain

As the rolling raindrops dance

To the rhythmic, clattering sounds!

The freshly fallen droplets of elixir

Drapes this mysterious earth

The emerald woods and charming flowers

Bloom as the monsoon rain quenches

The thirst of Mother Earth, take a moment

Amidst the chaos, adore the gentleness

Of the mirror drops crowning the leaves

Let this blissful monsoon rain

Dissolve the safely cocooned emotions

Echoing in casketed corners of heart

In the circle of season, monsoon rain is a
reason

For everything around you to re-emerge

This monsoon, let the life in you flourish.

34. Eternal Union

Cosmic whispers in the darkness

Through night's soft veil

Stars shining bright;

Stardust carries ancient secrets

I search within, moonlight

Illuminates my inner path

The world slows down

My heart expands

And as my spirit lifts

I realise, I am a part of

Something greater

35. Phases Of Life

The moon, a constant metamorphosis

A canvas of transformation

From darkness to radiant light

It evolves as a dynamic symbol

Changing its face and phase;

Like moon we rise and fall

Let our strength remain unbroken

Reminding us success and failures

Are fleeting moments

The full moon shines as a symbol

Of resilience and renewal.

36. The Space Between

As evening light dissolves,

Darkness descends

Enveloping the sky

A fragile war and hate entwine

Inner turmoil plucks the heartstrings

I retreat into my happiness

Yet, questions linger

Will time hold us together?

Are we doomed to fall apart?

Or will the cracks remain?

As a constant threat

Nothing lasts forever,

But some things....

Like the unsent letters

With words of emotions

Etched in every chamber of heart

Remain timeless...

37. Imprints

Time's relentless tide sweeps moments

Yet, memories are etched like fossils..

Hours vanish like sand between hands

Eternity's whisper fades

With each passing moment

Lost in the passage of memories

The first kiss, a last goodbye

Imprinted on heart, forever remain

Leaving echoes of what's past

Time's silent wings beat fast

Exposing moments, we can never forget

Moments dissolve like fleeting light

Yet in memory their lessons remain!

38. The Fragmented Heart

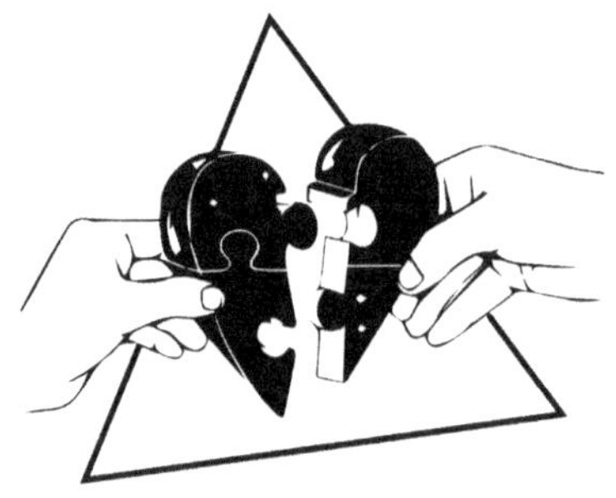

Subtle pain of tangled thoughts

Twisted beyond the threads of fate

I hear the quiet shatter

Of my conflicting desires

There was a season

When those little eyes

Sparkled with pure happiness..

The secret name unsaid aloud,

Seems never to be forgotten,

Caged in the corners of my heart

Still brings a feeble-crafted smile!

First love, often graced with innocence

And a hard goodbye!

Love, is it a human flaw?

Collecting my hopes and fears,

I ask myself only to realise

Everyone has fragmented memories,

And unfinished stories within..

39. The Present's Gift

In this present phase,

Your life unfolds with vibrant hue—

A gift unwrapped shining new

Let go of yesterday's memories,

Dear heart,

Welcome those blessings that never depart

As you step into this radiant day

May gratitude guide your way

Let every breath be filled with hope

And let life's vibrancy stir your

Deepest glee!

40. Shifting Colours

Humans wear their faces like masks, designed

To conceal emotions, and hide their mind

Smiles and frowns a wardrobe to display

Reflecting moods like changing seasons

They shed their skin like autumn leaves

Cutting ties with ease

Amidst chaos a few remain as

Unchanging constants, words are bonds

Rare and precious....

Yet, observing human nature

We learn trust is fragile

And can be easily impaired

Each thread of faith must be

Carefully woven as the

Broken fragments of trust

Never find their place..

41. The Weaver Of Time

God orchestrates life with perfect care

Our cries, He hears;

Our heart, He sees;

Answering prayers with divine ease

Though delayed

He guides our path, in darkness

We question His design

He whispers low

Just "Trust and align"

His light radiantly shines through

His love always grows

In humility, we understand

His mastery

Just trust His timings,

Infinitely wise.

42. Golden Awakening

Morning's glow, softly rises high

Bringing life to all below;

With warmth, earth revives

As golden rays thrive;

Reflecting its beauty

Ocean, sky, stars above

Mirror Sun's radiant love;

The Moon's pale glow

Echoes sunlight's dream

All shines bright, none compare

As the sunrise's splendour

Is beyond compare.

43. The Season Of Letting Go

Autumn's landscape, a crimson hue

Dried leaves rustle, beneath the footsteps

A reminder to release

What's worn and dried

Like fallen leaves

Our worries must shed

The weight of painful parts

This season is a work of noble art

A chance to heal,

Let go of burdens

To a lighter heart

And a brighter day.

44. Wildwood Wisdom

Beneath the forest's emerald light

Where the trees stand side by side

Their branches stretching and

Roots running deep;

The scent of pine and earth

Connect us to a life, profound

Their wisdom whispers secrets

Through the air; infusing us with life

The fragrance of trees, a healing breeze

Unlock the senses, renews our spirit

Nourishing hearts and calming minds

Gifting a new life, beyond our

Human disguise!

45. The Majestic Throne

The rugged landscapes stretch far and wide

A monument of nature's grand design..

From this height, the world unfolds

Inviting the brave, to conquer;

A breathtaking tapestry, a testament to time

The mountain, Earth's majestic throne

Fearless and free, yet steep and long

Humbles us with the possibilities that emerge

In awe, we pause

From the height, fear dissolves

In elevated state, we find clarity

Empowering us to conquer

The life's summits.

46. Sun-Kissed Sands

Yellow sand swirls like a golden sea

The Sun beats down, a fiery gaze

The brown breeze rustles

The grains of sand

Enduring through blazing days

The desert's beauty is harsh

Teaching resilience, adaptation,

To the human mind

Through rare desert flowers

Without a care, the thorny prickly arms

Of Cacti thrive; Camels roam

Majestic and slow in deserts lonely home

Where others can never belong..

47. Snow-Kissed Moments

The snow gently falls outside the window,

Carpeting the world in their

Mesmerising beauty;

As cold seeps in, I wrap

Myself in warmth and light;

Soft blankets envelop me

A good book, a cosy corner

A moment of peace;

I find my day in this simple joy

A sense of inner calmness,

These quiet moments are bliss

There is joy in stillness

As the world outside grows

Quiet and cold..

48. Sea Of Life

Rains of happiness and

Droplets of sorrows

Fill my ocean of life;

At times my soul is like

A wild bird that sings its own

Ballad of joy;

Now and then my heart is like

A wandering bird searching

For its own nest;

Just like everyone,

The story of my life

Is full of uncertainties

Yet, my life holds a purpose;

Every step leads to discovery

It's all about acceptance of reality

For a life unburdened

I wish to drop my anchor in the present

This unquenchable life calls forward,

I hope to sail in my ocean of life

Without sinking in regrets..

49. Light Within

In the battle of weakness and strength

Faith of hope is gifted

Yet, shadowed by the

Mysteries of agony and hate..

The spirit that can never be silenced, waits

Listen to those silent whispers to lift your soul

Keep hoping without fear, for

In the mirror, an inspiration you'll see..

With a glowing flame deep inside

Beaming with inner light

This flame guides you

Through life's beautiful passage

Illuminating the path

With a warm and gentle embrace!

Embrace its light in darkness

It will lead your way to

Celebrate life's fleeting states..

50. Silver Linings

Silver linings gift us with newfound light

Guiding us through life's complexities

Look above, and see the clouds drift by

Their gentle presence offers a ray of hope

Every cloud is a home, that drifts and stays

Within your heart, let peace remain

No matter where life's journey take you,

You are never lost

For home is within you.

As you turn the final page of this book,
believe that

You matter deeply. Just hold onto your worth.

You deserve love, light and happiness.

You are heard and valued.

Remember these words are not just for today,
but for every tomorrow

You matter and You are enough!

With immense gratitude, I thank you for
choosing Comforting Clouds!